Optimism and Joyful I₁

The Sixties Culture and Its Influence on British University Adult Education and the WEA

Roger Fieldhouse

Professor of Adult Education, University of Exeter

National Institute of Adult Continuing Education

First published in 1993 by the National Institute of Adult
Continuing Education (England and Wales) 19B De Montfort
Street, Leicester LE1 7GE
Company registration number 2603322
Charity registration number 1002775

British Library Cataloguing in Publication Data
A CIP record for this book is available from the British Library

ISBN 1 872941 37 0

Printed and bound in Great Britain by Echo Press, Loughborough

Contents

Preface

In August 1964 I arrived in North Yorkshire straight from university, to take up a post as tutor organiser for the Workers' Educational Association (WEA). Although I had just gained a postgraduate teaching qualification, my only adult education training was attendance at a week's summer school in Oxford. My only other qualifications were 24 years of life experience, a history degree and some good advice from my new boss, Fred Sedgwick, the WEA District Secretary. Thus equipped, together with a list of names and addresses of WEA branch secretaries and other potentially helpful contacts and a couple of ordnance survey maps, I set off one sunny August morning to explore that part of the Vale of York and the Pennine Dales where I was expected to promote and teach adult education classes for the WEA in return for £800 per annum.

I drove across the Vale of York from Northallerton to the ancient market town of Richmond, with its brooding Norman castle commanding the scarp above the River Swale and dominating the cobbled market place spread out in a horseshoe below its mighty keep. It was my first acquaintance with this small medieval town which I was later to come to know so well, and of which I was to write a history. After calling on the local WEA branch secretary, I drove on westwards into Swaledale, through Marsk, Grinton, Reeth, Healaugh and Low Row, until I came to a little bench by the side of the road, looking southwards over the dale. The sun was sparkling on the swift-flowing river below, and in the dale bottom the medley of tiny green fields, enclosed by their rugged dry-stone walls, formed an ancient, kaleidoscopic pattern. On the fellside opposite, the later enclosure walls climbed precipitously to the heather-clad summit. All was so quiet, almost totally quiet. Hardly a car passed; not a person was to be seen. The only movement was the occasional slow amble of the incredibly shaggy sheep grazing on the opposite fellside, and the dancing of the sunlit water in the river below.

I sat and slowly ate my sandwiches, and contemplated my good fortune. Was someone really going to pay me £800 a year to work in this beautiful countryside? Whatever has happened in the 30 years since that day, which has not all been so perfect, I shall always be grateful for, and never forget, my initiation into adult education in the Yorkshire Dales.

This research project investigating the influence of the sixties culture on adult education has been a pleasant return to that lost age. I am grateful to what was the Universities Funding Council for making a grant towards the cost of carrying out the research, and to the hundred or so 'sixties people' who responded to my questionnaire, and particularly the 15 who further agreed to be interviewed. I wish also to thank Tom Steele for conducting some of the interviews and analysing the responses about people's cultural interests (pp 7–12); Sue Milward for converting much of the raw material in the questionnaires into meaningful tables, and Greta Tink, who patiently converts my scribblings into word-processed text, and then equally patiently incorporates my later alterations.

Ultimately, as always, the author must accept responsibility for what appears in print, and for all interpretations and expressions of view. Any fault is mine alone.

ROGER FIELDHOUSE
Exeter, March 1993

Introduction

This publication describes the political, social and cultural profile of a sample of entrants to the profession of adult education in British universities or the Workers' Educational Association (WEA) during the period 1965–75. It examines the extent to which this sample brought aspects of the sixties political culture with them into adult education and whether this political culture influenced their attitudes to their work and their expectations of what they might achieve through the medium of adult education. It summarises their views on the purpose of adult education, their adult education priorities, their opinions of the 1973 Russell Report and the extent to which a commitment to socially purposive adult education brought them into conflict with their employers or paymasters.

In 1961–2 a comparable survey was carried out under the auspices of the then active Tutors' Association and the Department of Adult Education of Manchester University. [1] One of the respondents to that survey commented that 'before my generation of adult tutors fades away an enquiry should be held into the change in adult education, i.e. from avowed social objectives (emancipation of the working class) to present background'. [2] The current survey pursues that objective, examining the political, social and cultural nature of the universities/WEA adult education of the sixties and early seventies, from an historical perspective. Where appropriate it will make comparisons with the 1961–2 survey. It also provides an opportunity to identify the ideological changes which have taken place in British universities/WEA adult education during the last two decades.

This survey is based on a questionnaire distributed in February 1992 to 340 people who entered British university adult education or extramural departments or the WEA between c.1965–75, together with 15 interviews. [3] The questionnaire consisted of 19 sections eliciting personal details and information about social background, religious and political affiliations, trade union activity, membership of organisations and societies, newspapers and journals read, attitudes to a range of political issues, General Election voting, involvement in political activities, ideological position, cultural interests, adult education priorities, perceived political or social purposes of adult education, reaction to the Russell Report, employers' attitudes, other constraints (if any) experienced in adult education work, and any other relevant information. The questionnaire concentrated on the period of the respondents' first adult education post, although a few questions were asked about present-day attitudes to enable comparisons to be made.

All university adult education/extra-mural departments and WEA districts had previously been asked for names and addresses of present or past staff who had entered adult education during the period 1965–75. All those so identified were sent a questionnaire. Where departments or districts had not supplied this information, a batch of questionnaires was sent to the head of department or district secretary with a request to distribute them to appropriate people. A hundred and three questionnaires were returned, of which 16 proved to be invalid (mainly because the respondent had not begun his or her adult education career within the period being studied). The remaining 87 constitute the sample, representing a 25 per cent return. Fifty-seven per cent of the sample began their adult education work during the 1960s and 43 per cent between 1970 and 1976. Fifty-three per cent started work as university teachers (plus 4.7 per cent in administration) and 33 per cent began in the WEA. The remainder started their adult education life in a variety of other ways – in local authority further or community education, in a college of education or as a part-time tutor, subsequently moving into a university or the WEA.

The question inevitably arises: how truly representative is this sample? The same question was asked by the author of the 1961–2 survey. He concluded that more deeply committed tutors were more likely to take the trouble and find interest in replying to a questionnaire and that 'it is reasonable to suppose that left-wing tutors are more ready to participate in social enquiries' because of the historical association of the Left with social enquiry in general. Therefore there was assumed to be an element of self-selective bias in the survey. [4] The same is still likely to be true today. One university director replied: 'I think all of us would be reluctant to be surveyed; we are a rather practical department and ideological/political tendencies are not a feature of our memory of those years'. However, he went on to say that he was 'conscious that if your sample reaches only the "ideologically/politically" interested then your research will be skewed and flawed', and therefore requested copies of the questionnaire to distribute. However, none was returned from that department.

Other stated reasons for not responding were that it was too time-consuming ('Time is money, as they say, these days more than ever ....'); that the questions were too intrusive; and that the promised confidentiality could not be relied upon. One deputy director replied to say that he could not complete the questionnaire because he considered 'the information ... too sensitive, capable of being misinterpreted, lacking in assurance of confidentiality ...'. He felt that 'at the present time in particular, data is so insecure that I would not feel confident that the information can necessarily be guaranteed to remain confidential'. This fear relates to the concern expressed by two other university lecturers about the real intentions of the Universities Funding Council in funding this research project.

As one of them stated: 'almost whatever answers were forthcoming, the data would have an explosive effect in the current educational climate. I cannot imagine what purpose the UFC might have in exploring the political allegiances of one (already very vulnerable) section of university staff'. [5]

An almost identical point was made by a WEA district secretary who expressed concern about the kinds of information the survey would collate. 'The problem is that the information brought together – particularly for a body like the WEA, which is always exposed – could be very politically sensitive if it got into mischievous hands'. He was not confident that it could be kept out of such hands, and therefore advised his district secretary colleagues not to co-operate. This closely mirrored the WEA's attitude in 1961–2, when the district secretaries' meeting then felt unable to help with the distribution of questionnaires. [6] Despite reassurances about confidentiality, and an agreement not to identify the WEA separately from the universities, this advice led to the relatively few returns from WEA personnel.

There were thus three main reasons for not responding to the questionnaire: (1) insufficient time; (2) a pragmatic disposition which distrusts or discounts sociological or ideological surveys; (3) fear of the political use to which such information might be put in the present climate. Whereas the first can apply indiscriminately across the political spectrum, the second is more likely to apply to those in the political centre, whereas the third is most likely to be felt by the more politically committed – particularly on the Left. Therefore, to some extent, these negative influences do balance each other out.

A more serious methodological problem is validating people's memories of the past. Apart from the normal fallibilities of memory, there is the political filter which causes or enables people to forget the political commitments and actions of their youth. There may be a tendency to minimise (either consciously or unconsciously) some more extreme political attitudes, especially in these New Times. Those sections in the questionnaire, which ask for a comparison between 'then' and 'now' were intended to jog people's memories into a more accurate recollection. The interviews were a further check on this distortion. But if anything, there will be a tendency to belittle the political extremism of 20 years ago.

part one

The Sixties Culture and a Sample of Adult Educators

The Sixties Political Culture

The 'sixties political culture' which the 87 respondents experienced at the time they began their work in adult education was a complex amalgam of optimism, change and protest. Even if the specific views and beliefs that collectively made up this political culture were not shared by a majority, they were nevertheless very influential in forming political attitudes, particularly among young people, at that time.

As one historian of the period has remarked, 'generalising about "the mood of the country" is the stock-in-trade of journalists; historians should know better ... Yet when all the qualifications and exceptions have been totted up, it is not unfair to speak of there being an optimism abroad in British Society during the sixties'.[7] There was a 'joyful irreverence' which affected particularly those in their teens and twenties – the age of the subjects of this survey. Even if it was a 'false optimism' it was a powerful influence. It led to a widespread belief in ever-improving social conditions, and the possibility of really changing society.

The changes that were actually (or were believed to be) taking place encompassed the replacement of class barriers by ever-more-rapid social mobility and, particularly after the Labour election victory of 1964, the rise of a meritocracy and the dawn of a new technological age: a New Britain. The contribution which education was expected to play in effecting this social change was enormous, building on the Robbins and Newsome Reports of 1963. The Plowden Report (1967), the great comprehensive debates of the later 1960s and the establishment of the Open University in 1969 were further manifestations of this phenomenon, as indeed was the Russell Report of 1973.

Alongside this supposed social revolution another was apparently taking place in moral attitudes. Although rampant sexual permissiveness was something of a myth, social surveys such as Geoffrey Gorer's *Sex and Marriage in England Today* (1971) did reveal clear signs of a definite trend away from older social controls. [8] There was also a strong sense that work was not the be-all and end-all of life: there were other, higher goals to aim for than just a good job.

The protest culture also derived from the rejection of what were considered out-moded values. These were largely political. Support for CND had been strong in the early sixties, but became more muted after the election of a Labour Government in 1964 and the creation of a Ministry of Disarmament (however cynical that really was). Conversely, support for the Anti-Apartheid Movement and against a sell-out over Rhodesia increased in the late 1960s, as did anti-racism, particularly after the formation of the National Front in 1966 and Enoch Powell's infamous 'rivers of blood' speech against immigration in 1968. These, together with the introduction of a restrictive Race Relations Act in the same year, all gave a focus to opposition to racism.

On the industrial front, vociferous protests were made about the Labour Government's prices and incomes policy and the wage-freeze imposed in 1966. However justified by economic crisis, these caused widespread resentment because they ran counter to working-class and left-wing expectations of the new Government. Industrial disputes began to proliferate: in 1967 there were 2,116 disputes and over 2.7 million working days lost. In 1969 the number of disputes rose to 3,116 and over 6.8 million working days were lost. [9] Protests concentrated on the Government's 1969 White Paper, *In Place of Strife*, and the Industrial Relations Bills unsuccessfully introduced later that year, which aimed to drastically restrict trade union activities and withdraw the immunity of unofficial strikers from legal sanctions. [10] As a young WEA tutor organiser, appointed in 1966, Neil Kinnock helped to lead the opposition in South Wales to *In Place of Strife*. [11] Protests continued in the seventies to the Heath Government's Industrial Relations Act (1971), leading to increasing industrial action and culminating in the three-day-week and the miners' strike of 1974. Much of this opposition to Government industrial relations policy was based on the belief in greater workers' control. The Institute of Workers' Control had close links with adult education at that time.

Another focus of protest was the Anti-Vietnam War campaign which formed a nucleus of the student protest movement of 1968. Although less powerful than the student protests in France and the US, the British students, particularly at Essex University and the LSE, organised pro-tests against the conservative tendencies of higher education as well as the Vietnam War, racism and the activities of far-Right groups in Britain.

There were also protests about the retreat from the original principle of a free health service and universalism as the basis of social welfare. In particular there was anger about the 'poverty-trap' caused by the introduction of means-tested supplementary benefits in 1966, and the reintroduction of medical prescription and dental charges in 1968.

But not all the protests of the sixties came from political activist students or trade unionists. There was increasing community action taken by previously unpoliticised social groups against local or central govern-ment plans which they disliked, and, on a very different stage, there were the anti-social protests of the Mods and Rockers rampaging through popular holiday resorts.

This complex web of optimism, change and protest created a political culture which was imbibed by those who entered adult education as tutors or organisers in the late sixties and early seventies. One of those who did begin his adult education work then has more recently captured the flavour of that time (and the intervening change!):

We've become decent, established, stable
Able enough, our path defined and finite
Well within the Pale
We no longer rail against humdrum limitation
Except quietly, in committee and a memo ...

We moved from 'Flower-Power' to Power Ploys
From Joy to Jargon

From 'doing it in the road'
To keeping a Neighbourhood Watch.
We gave Peace a chance
Now little's left to chance.

The 'New Age'
is Another Age.
We moved from Innocence
To Commonsense
From 'Be-ins' to
'Has-beens' with accreditation ...[12]

A Sample of Adult Educators

The survey sample of 87 respondents consisted of 76 men and 11 women, which probably reflects the gender balance of professionals in university adult education and the WEA in the sixties and seventies reasonably accurately. As already mentioned, over half were employed by the universities and a third by the WEA. The remainder occupied a miscellany of posts, including part-time ones. They moved to a university or the WEA subsequently. Although the vast majority were teachers, or combined teaching with organising, five of the sample were administrators in their first adult education post.

Their Educational Background

Of the 74 respondents who answered the question about their primary school, approximately three-quarters had attended local authority schools and a quarter fee-paying junior or preparatory schools. Compared with the national figure of 95 per cent of primary pupils attending public sector schools, [13] there was a considerable over-representation of ex-private school pupils in the sample.

A similarly privileged picture emerges of the respondents' secondary

4

schooling. Fifteen per cent had been to public schools and another 10 per cent to grant-aided or direct grant schools, compared with the 1969 national figure for Great Britain of six per cent of pupils at independent secondary schools and 3.5 per cent at assisted schools. [14] Most of the remainder (over two-thirds of the whole sample) attended a selective grammar school or Scottish (selective) high school, compared with the national average of 23 per cent. [15] Conversely, only 5.7 per cent had attended a secondary modern school, 2.3 per cent a technical school and 3.4 per cent a comprehensive school, whereas nationally two-thirds of all children attended such schools. [16] Two of the sample (2.2 per cent) had been educated abroad. [17]

However, apart from the rather high proportion of ex-'public' and grant-aided school pupils, it is not really surprising that a majority were educated in the upper reaches of the 1944 tripartite system, given that the jobs they were doing were academic ones.

This picture of secondary schooling in fact corresponds almost exactly with that of the 1961–2 survey, where 68 per cent came from grammar schools, 16.3 per cent from public schools, 12.7 per cent from elementary schools and three per cent from 'other' schools. [18]

After school, two of the respondents (2.3 per cent) had gone on initially to further education, 15 per cent attended a college, 4.6 per cent a polytechnic (these came into existence only after 1967), but all except one of the sample completed their education at a university. (There is an overlap in these categories because some people progressed from one post-school institution to another.) Over one-third of the sample attained a doctorate by the time they had finished their education and another 21 per cent obtained masters' degrees of one kind or another. A further 13 per cent gained a teaching certificate or diploma, which meant that well over two-thirds of the sample had postgraduate qualifications, but a relatively small number were qualified to teach! The remainder consisted of 27 per cent with a BA degree but only 3.5 per cent with a BSc, reflecting the arts bias in adult education. One person was qualified with a Dip.Tech.

Social Class

The social background of the sample was measured by their assessment of the social class of their fathers and mothers and themselves when they first started in adult education, and their social class today. Table 1.1 shows the responses of those who answered these questions. (About one-sixth of the sample did not answer about their parents, but most answered about themselves.)

Table 1.1 Assessed social class

Assessed social class	Father	Mother	Self when starting AE	Self today
	%	%	%	%
Upper middle class	5.4	5.6	3.6	13.6
Middle class	27.0	27.8	67.9	69.1
Lower middle class	20.3	26.4	14.3	9.9
Skilled working class	24.3	13.9	8.3	4.9
Semi/unskilled working class	23.0	26.4	6.0	2.5
Total	**100.00**	**100.00**	**100.00**	**100.00**

The most significant fact about this distribution is that whereas it is fairly evenly spread as far as parental background is concerned, it is a very different distribution as far as the respondents themselves are concerned. These grammar school and university-educated young people were part of the sixties socially mobile meritocracy. In considerable numbers they felt that they had risen into the ranks of the middle class by virtue of their education and/or professionalisation. It is also noticeable that this trend has continued as they got older – more of them feeling they have moved further up the social ladder into the middle or upper-middle class by the present day.

There is a very marked contrast between the self-assessment of this sample of (then) young adult educationists and the 1961–2 sample, only

23 per cent of whom assessed themselves as middle or upper-middle class, 34 per cent as lower-middle class, 34 per cent as upper-working and nine per cent as lower-working class. [19] The difference is explained by the different age profile of the 1961–2 sample, which was all-age. As Ruddock says, 'over the age of 45 the tutor's origin appears more likely to be working class'. [20] The younger generation coming into adult education in the sixties and seventies was drawn extensively from the same working class or lower-middle class background as far as their parents were concerned, but they themselves very largely felt they had moved away from their class origins. In the process, British university and WEA adult education was losing its traditional close links with the working class. It was being infiltrated by the post-1944 eleven-plus victors: the new meritocrats with rather different loyalties, and social and political views shaped more by their education than their class origins.

Religion

Another sign of the changing times was that nearly three-quarters of the respondents were not active members of any church or religious sect. This probably corresponds with the 1961–2 impression 'that tutors in general have less religious commitment than other people of similar educational attainment'. [21]

Of the 26 per cent who were religiously active, half were Anglican and the others a smattering of Methodists and Catholics, and one Baptist, Quaker, Welsh Reform Church, and 'Christian'.

Cultural Interests

Respondents were invited to indicate their cultural interests in the sixties and seventies by listing a film or film director, a novel or author, a play or playwright and type of music that was particularly important to, or influential on, them at that time. [22]

Of the 72 responses about films, two-thirds responded positively.

The remainder had no particular interest in film. There were 20 named films, while the rest named directors only. Of those who answered positively 33 per cent named British directors or films, almost all known for their political and social commentary. They were very much centred on the fifties and sixties social realist films of Reisz, Richardson, Attenborough and Loach – *The Loneliness of the Long Distance Runner, Saturday Night, Sunday Morning, Oh, What a Lovely War, Billy Liar* – which in turn leant on the fifties paperback fictions of working class life. Grierson the documentary maker was the only non-contemporary mentioned.

Seven respondents named Hollywood directors and films. Of these most had political and social commentary and several, including *Dr Strangelove, Easy Rider, One Flew Over the Cuckoo's Nest*, were quite cultish. Only two seemed to belong to a different era and, perhaps, sensibility – Wilder's *Seven Year Itch* and Ford's *Grapes of Wrath* – though both are classics and rich in social comment.

A remarkable interest was shown in European directors. Of the 26 directors named by respondents 14 were European. The most popular director (6) was Ingmar Bergman, well-known for Scandinavian angst and deep philosophising. Truffaut and Eisenstein got three votes each (along with Russell and by inference Milosz Forman whose film *One Flew Over the Cuckoo's Nest* was mentioned by three people). There was a wide range of interests: Pasolini's Italian poetic anti-catholicism, the French new wave (Resnais, Goddard, Truffaut), the Spanish anarchist surrealist Buñuel, the Polish Marxist Varda (*Ashes and Diamonds*), Costa-Gavros's anti-Greek colonels *Z* and the Czech Jiri Mendel's anarchistic anti-communist *Closely Observed Trains*. The classic *Potemkin* was the only non-contemporary film mentioned and Tatti the only comic director.

Overall there was a relatively high interest in film and, by those who responded positively, high awareness of contemporary film in Britain, Hollywood and Europe. Virtually all the films mentioned displayed a high level of 'anti-establishment' feeling, reflecting revolutionary, working class, sub-cultural, deviant and/or psychologically disturbed viewpoints. There was a notable 'literary' quality to many of the films mentioned, many having been developed from popular novels. Most of the European films are, however, visually stunning and quite experimental, as are some of the British and American films. Most were by young directors or, like Buñuel, directors coming out of exile and obscurity. There was no mention of Indian, Chinese or other third world cinema, no women directors except Varda and no films dealt with race, ethnicity or feminism.

Seventy-four people responded to the question about novels or authors, of whom eight expressed no interest, 46 mentioned individual authors and 17 mentioned titles of books. The 46 authors included 25 who were British, eight American, two Irish, two Australian and seven European (probably in translation). Only six were women and 13 are no longer living. Six were non-fiction writers. The most popular authors (although they receive only four mentions each) were Hardy, Heller and Orwell (all novelists), with *Catch 22* getting four mentions. Sillitoe, Lawrence, Murdoch and Bellow each got three mentions. There was a very wide range of interest, with no single author dominating. *Catch 22* was probably widely read, given that it was mentioned four times by name. If so, it represents a widespread scepticism about official attitudes, perhaps even a mild psychopathology about intentions, since there is no way out of the bureaucratic trap. The breadth of the rest of the response could indicate how broad English literary culture was at the time and how many slight differences of emphasis it could contain. Nevertheless some concentration around novels of social realism and social criticism can be identified, with a small interest in feminism and a slightly larger one in European novels, especially Russian. Contemporary novelists are well represented, including some of the angry young men but excluding Amis and Osborne and most of the northern working class 'kitchen sink' writers except Barstow, on whose work several of the chosen films were based. Only one (dead) poet (Donne) was mentioned and one playwright (Wesker). Of the six non-fiction writers mentioned, there were two Marxist historians (Thompson and Hobsbawm), one American economist (Galbraith), one Australian feminist (Greer), one Marxist theorist

(Marcuse) and one radical cleric (Huddleston). The selection is again almost entirely white Euro-American male, with few women and only one black (Baldwin).

There were 72 responses to the question about music. These span a wide range, although quite a high proportion (21 per cent) showed no interest in music at all. Classical, which included symphonic, chamber, opera, modern and church music, was mentioned 30 times (42 per cent), then came folk, which included folk-rock, protest and blues, 21 (29 per cent), followed by rock (i.e. Zappa, Floyd, Stones, Hendrix, The Doors and 'progressive', etc.) 16 (22 per cent) and jazz, including mainstream, modern and traditional, 10 (14 per cent) and finally pop, (i.e. dance, easy listening and standards) with five adherents (7 per cent).

There is always a problem about music categories since, for example, most modern jazz fans cannot stand traditional jazz and vice versa, while the line between pop and rock is largely arbitrary and blues could equally mean some rock (e.g. Hendrix). If folk, rock and pop were added together, that became the biggest category at 42 (58 per cent). But the wide range is again interesting, showing just how broad musical culture was with 37 different responses from the 72 respondents. The biggest single option was 'classical' as a genre at 15 (21 per cent) followed by Bob Dylan at nine (13 per cent), the Stones at five (7 per cent) and then Simon and Garfunkel and the Beatles on two each (3 per cent), the latter perhaps surprisingly low down the list.

Of 'classical' music, opera got three mentions (only Verdi by name) and modern, though not contemporary, music got five (Bartok, Stravinsky, Mahler, Sibelius and 'twentieth century'). Symphonic, mostly nineteenth century, included Beethoven and Schubert only and no Mozart, Haydn, or Mendelssohn, for example. Baroque got two votes, though.

Generally the selection is what might be expected of sixties students with a wide range of interests. There were none of the slightly more cultish things like Incredible String Band or Albinoni, which shows that not very many were on the outer fringes of musical culture. As in the novel and film sections, social criticism and protest was noticeable – folk did as well as rock and pop combined, for example (which may show a preference for bohemianism and bitter rather than dope and dancing!). There was also a noticeable interest in serious music, which would include not only 'classical' but also modern jazz, blues, some folk, especially Dylan, and arguably some rock. White male European and American music predominated, with some black representation in blues and rock but nothing 'ethnic' like Missa Luba or what would now be called 'world music', and no distinguishable feminist music.

Of the 76 who responded to the question about plays or playwrights, a large number, 32 (44 per cent) showed no interest at all. Of the rest, a wide range of authors was chosen. Of these, 18 (67 per cent) were British, the most popular being Shakespeare with five, Wesker with four and, perhaps surprisingly, John McGrath of 7/84 Theatre Company with four. Arthur Miller, the modern American playwright, also got two mentions. Only three playwrights were European, Dario Fo, Brecht and Weiss. Two women, Delaney and Littlewood, were mentioned, but no black writers at all.

Of the plays named *The Cheviot and the Stag ...* (McGrath, 7/84), and *Taking Our Time* (Red Ladder) were seventies agit prop theatre, *Occupations* was about Gramsci (Griffiths), *Accidental Death of an Anarchist* (Dario Fo) was about police/fascist brutality and *Marat Sade* (Weiss) about revolution in a madhouse, showing a strong Left orientation. *Oh, What a Lovely War* (Littlewood/Theatre Workshop) was anti-war, O'Casey's *Juno and the Paycock* a satire on Irish nationalism and *Richard III* about political intrigue. *Who's Afraid of Virginia Woolf?* (Albee) is psycho-drama, *Royal Hunt of the Sun* (Shaffer) is about the Spanish conquest of Mexico and *A Man for All Seasons* (Bolt) about Thomas Moore and Henry VIII. Many of these were also made into films, so there might be some misplacement here. But they all go to show a strong political and psychological (psychopathic?) interest. A surprisingly large number were contemporary, and only Eliot and Williams seem to belong to an earlier period (Shakespeare and Brecht must by now be deemed 'classic'). The great majority of the authors were politically left-wing and many, like Griffiths, Loach, Allen and Potter, are probably best known for their television work. It is quite likely that although the survey shows an interest in contemporary theatre, there was not in fact much theatre-going and that much of what was seen may well have been through such other media as film and TV. There was some awareness of avant-garde theatre like Bond, but much more the sense of drama as part of a broader political culture rather than interest in it as an art form as such. There was no expressed interest in comedy shows, musicals or light drama – it was all very serious.

Answers about all four genres seem to indicate a largely political, intellectual culture of the centre and left with little interest in light, popular or comic work on the one hand, (i.e. middle-brow culture) or in the cutting edge of avant-garde work on the other (i.e. high-brow). There was some feeling for popular culture in music, at least, and in some books but on the whole a rather puritan selection of serious and worthy work spiced by revolutionary and psychopathological elements, which probably indicate membership of a culture rather than specific interest in the art forms as such. However, the interest is lively and critical of the 'establishment' (a sixties word) – and celebrates working class and deviant, but not women's or 'ethnic' viewpoints.

Ideological Position

The political awareness revealed in the respondents' cultural interests is also reflected in their responses to a range of political questions. In 1961–2 it was noted that: 'The commonest political position recorded by tutors is Moderate Left ... Younger tutors, as might be expected, tend more to the Far positions, though even in the youngest group twice as many take a Moderate or Centre one'. [23] A very similar picture emerges from a collation of the responses in the current survey relating to attitudes to positive discrimination in social policy and to the importance of equality of opportunity, together with respondents' own assessment of their ideological position and their General Election voting pattern between 1964–74. Two-thirds of the sample fall into a broadly centrist political category (from Liberal to moderate Labour); nearly a quarter were further to the left and 10 per cent further to the right.

Table 1.2 shows the respondents' own recollection of their ideological position in the late sixties or early seventies, with its heavy concentration on social democratic and Labourist positions.

Table 1.2 Ideological position in late sixties/early seventies

	No.	*%*
Conservative	8	9.4
Liberal	2	2.4
Social democratic	18	21.2
Labourist	29	34.1
Democratic socialist	1	1.2
Socialist	2	2.4
Marxist	11	12.9
Trotskyist	4	4.7
Anarchist	3	3.5
Feminist	3	3.5
Ecologist	1	1.2
Radical	1	1.2
Scottish Nationalist	1	1.2
Welsh Nationalist	1	1.2
Not stated	2	–
Total	**87**	**100.00**

Of course, compared with the population as a whole, this sample is hugely under-representative of the Right and greatly over-representative both of the centre and, particularly, the Left. But as explained earlier, the sample is unlikely to be politically skewed to any significant degree. Indeed, if anything, it exaggerates the centrism at the expense of the political extremes. Therefore it is reasonable to assume that this ideological orientation is an approximate reflection of the politics of university/WEA adult education professionals at that time. They were considerably more Labourist/social democratic than the total population and had a much greater proportion of Left-inclined people. Conversely, Conservatism was present to a much smaller degree than in the total population, to the extent of its being a minority influence.

Political Activities

This ideological orientation is, not surprisingly, reflected in membership of political parties or political organisations. Only 2.3 per cent of the sample (two people) belonged to the Conservative Party but 34 people (39 per cent) belonged to the Labour Party. No one belonged to the Liberal Party but there was one member each of the Co-operative Party and the Irish SDLP (2.3 per cent), three Communist party members (3.4 per cent), six members of the Trotskyist International Socialists (6.9 per cent), and one each of the Trotskyist Socialist Labour League and International Marxists (2.3 per cent), together with one member of the Socialist Party of Great Britain (1.1 per cent) and three members of Anarchist groups (3.4 per cent). Over 50 per cent of the sample claimed membership of a political party or organisation at that time. This suggests a very high level of active political party membership compared with the tiny proportion of the national adult population who were active members either of the major political parties or of the minority parties and organisations on the far Left, where total membership was extremely small. [24] Membership was also significantly higher than the one-third recorded in the 1961-2 survey, [25] again reflecting the different age profile of the two samples.

The general centre-left political orientation of the sample is again reflected in the voting pattern in the general elections between 1964 and 1974 (shown in Table 1.3).

Table 1.3 Votes cast in General Elections

	1964	1966	1970	1974 (Feb)	1974 (Oct)
No. of valid cases*	62	74	77	79	79
	Percentage of total votes cast				
Conservative	11.3	9.5	9.00	11.4	11.4
Liberal	6.5	4.0	7.8	13.9	11.4
Labour	79.0	82.5	79.3	69.6	72.2
ILP	–	–	1.3	–	–
SDLP	–	–	1.3	3.8	3.8
Scottish Nationalist	–	1.3	1.3	1.3	1.3
Spoiled paper	3.2	2.7	–	–	–
Total	**100.00**	**100.00**	**100.00**	**100.00**	**100.00**

* (excluding those who did not vote or who were not eligible)

The swings to and from Labour approximately reflect the national voting pattern – the narrow Labour victory of 1964, the increased majority of 1966, the unexpected Conservative victory on a low vote in 1970, the hung parliament of February 1974 (with increased Liberal and Nationalist representation and a larger actual vote for Conservative than for Labour), and the tiny Labour majority of October 1974. But the proportion of Labour voters over this 10-year period, fluctuating between 70 and 80 per cent, compares with a national Labour vote of below 36 per cent (October 1974) to 46 per cent (1970). [26]

There was also a relatively high incidence of trade union membership: 55 per cent. Quite a number of people belonged to more than one trade union, or moved from one to another and recorded dual membership. Most people belonged to teaching unions of one kind or another. Fifty per cent of the total sample belonged to the Association of University Teachers (AUT), 4.5 per cent to the Association of Tutors in Adult

Education (which was in decline by this date) and 2.3 per cent to the WEA's Tutors' Association. A fifth of the sample belonged to the left-wing scientific workers' union, ASTMS, which was actively recruiting members in the field of education at that time. There was a 10 per cent membership of schoolteachers' unions and 6.8 per cent membership of NATFHE. There was also a sizable membership of the TGWU (8 per cent) and a smattering of membership of various other non-teaching trade unions, including NALGO, NUPE and TASS.

A third of the trade union members held office of some kind (branch officer, council delegate, member of executive, etc.), which reflects a fairly high degree of trade union activism.

There was also considerable involvement in other organisations or movements, which reveals how adult education was intimately connected with the 'change or protest' culture. A quarter of the sample belonged to CND or other peace organisations and 37 per cent claimed to have been actively involved in the peace movement. A quarter of the sample were active in the anti-racist movement and 28 per cent in the anti-Vietnam War movement. The women's movement was less well supported (17 per cent), but considering that the sample was predominantly male, this represents a high level of involvement. Other organisations which people belonged to included the Anti-Apartheid Movement (8 per cent), the Fabian Society (3.4 per cent) and the British Association of Social Workers (2.3 per cent) and there was the odd member of Amnesty International, the Third World Group, the Anti-Nazi League, the Institute of Workers' Control, the Society of Industrial Tutors, the British Society for Social Responsibility in Science, a Labour Club, a Trades Council and a local New Left Group. Some 15 per cent of the sample held office of some kind in one or more of these organisations. Together with the political party and trade union involvement, it does add up to a high active involvement in the sixties social or political movements campaigning for change or protesting about government or international activities.

When asked to summarise briefly their main political activities in the sixties or early seventies, nearly half did not respond or said they had none. Comments included:

I am not a political activist.
I'm a non-joiner.
Disillusioned by politics and politicians.
Too busy doing other things.

However, 53 per cent of the sample did attempt to summarise their political activities. Some mentioned just one, but others listed several activities. Far and away the most common was active politics on behalf of the Labour Party (mentioned 21 times) and other political activity for more left-wing groups (9 times). Successful or unsuccessful candidacy in local government elections was referred to five times.

The other major activity was direct action, demonstrations and marches on behalf of a wide variety of mainly leftist causes, including the anti-Vietnam War campaign, CND and the peace movement, anti-apartheid, anti-racism, the anti-imperialist struggle and women's rights. Such direct action was mentioned 15 times. Many people were involved in several of these campaigns. As one respondent expressed it, 'you name it and I was probably there'. Closely related to these activities were the following: student politics (mentioned four times), opposition to the Government's industrial relations policy (2), defending the trade union movement (1), promoting workers' control (1), opposing or dealing with the consequences of unemployment (2), solidarity with the miners (1), civil rights in Northern Ireland (2), equal opportunities (2), promoting career opportunities for women (1) and women/church issues (1).

There were also a number of more specific activities relating to particular individuals' interests, and therefore mostly mentioned only once. These included working in education as a liberating or political activity, educational work with ethnic minorities, improving education, politicising social work, involvement in the child care movement, community work, political journalism, promoting social responsibility in science, supporting the environment movement and nature conservation.

17

Newspaper Readership

The political tendencies, interests and activities of these adult education-ists were, not surprisingly, reflected in (or shaped or reinforced by) the newspapers and journals that they read.

Tables 1.4 and 1.5 summarise the respondents' newspaper reading habits and compare these with the 1961–2 survey [27] and the national pattern of the sixties and seventies. The 1961–2 and the current surveys both add up to more than 100 per cent because a number of respondents read more than one daily or Sunday newspaper. The national daily circulation figures are calculated as a percentage of those listed by the Central Office of Information in 1976, [28] and the national Sunday circulation is similarly calculated from an analysis by Raymond Williams in 1967. [29]

Table 1.4 Daily Newspaper Readership

Newspaper	% of sample	% of 61–2 survey	% of national circulation (Jan–Dec 75)
Guardian	80.5	61.2	2.1
Times	18.4	29.4	2.2
Daily Worker/ Morning Star	9.2	2.9	0.3
Daily Telegraph	8.0	14.7	9.2
Financial Times	4.6	1.2	1.2
Scotsman	4.6	0.0	0.6
Glasgow Herald	2.3	0.0	0.7
Daily Mail	1.1	7.0	12.1
Daily Mirror	1.1	1.2	27.6
Daily Herald	1.1	8.8	Closed
Irish News	1.1	0.0	N/K
Daily Express	0.0	4.1	19.4
Sun	0.0	0.0	24.5

Table 1.5 Sunday Newspaper Readership

Newspaper	% of sample	% of 61–2 sample	% of national circulation (67)
Observer	69.0	64.7	3.2
Sunday Times	42.5	24.1	4.9
Sunday Telegraph	4.6	5.9	2.5
Sunday Mirror	2.3	0.0	19.1
Sunday Express	1.1	9.4	15.9
Scottish Sunday Mail	1.1	0.0	2.7
Sunday Citizen/ Reynolds News	0.0	3.5	0.9
News of the World	0.0	0.6	23.5
The People	0.0	0.0	21.0
Scottish Sunday Post	0.0	0.0	6.3

Apart from the expected unpopularity of the tabloids compared with the national readership pattern, what stands out is the massive popularity of the *Guardian* and, to a slightly less extent, the *Observer*. Also of considerable popularity were the *Sunday Times* and *The Times* and, given its small national circulation, the Communist *Daily Worker*, which became the *Morning Star* in 1966. Considering the educational background and social class of the sample, the *Telegraph* was not widely read – again reflecting the general political orientation of the respondents.

The main difference between the 1961–2 survey and the current one was the greater popularity of the *Guardian*, the *Sunday Times* and the *Daily Worker/Morning Star* by 1965–75. To some extent this may reflect the younger age-group (less inclined to read papers like the *Mail* or *Express*); partly the demise of the *Herald* and the switch of its readership to other papers; but also the growing strength of the *Guardian* as a truly national newspaper.

The journals listed in the questionnaire are given in Table 1.6 in the order of their popularity.

Table 1.6 Journals read regularly

	% of sample
New Statesman	48.3
New Society	39.1
Private Eye	27.6
Economist	17.2
New Left Review	17.2
New Scientist	14.9
Marxism Today	12.6
Spectator	8.0
Spare Rib	8.0
Black Dwarf	6.9
Encounter	4.6

In 1961–2, the *New Statesman* was read by 34.7 per cent of those surveyed. [30]

Other journals which were specified by more than one respondent in the current survey were *Tribune* (5.7 per cent), *Socialist Worker* (4.6 per cent), *The Times Literary Supplement* (2.3 per cent) and *Social Work Today* (2.3 per cent). Others which were mentioned by one respondent each included *Feminist Review, Newsweek, Time Magazine, She, British Journal of Social Work, Geographical Magazine, UNESCO Courier, Investors Chronicle, International Socialism, Oz* and *Spokesman*. Strangely, the *Listener*, which was read by more than a third of the 1961–2 sample, [31] was not mentioned by anyone in the current survey.

Even allowing for the vagaries of memory, it is quite clear that the 'quality' and liberal/left-wing press and journals constituted the main newspaper and journal reading of the young adult educators in the sixties and seventies.

Political and Social Attitudes

Finally, their recollected attitude to a number of important political and social issues of that time was recorded on a five-point scale, from strong disagreement to strong agreement. The responses are summarised in Table 1.7. Well over four-fifths of the sample conceived of Britain as being a class-divided society in the sixties and seventies, and three-quarters regarded racial divisions as a major problem. But less than half felt that male chauvinism was such a problem: over a third were indifferent or undecided about this issue.

In their views about social policy, nearly everyone believed that it should be based on equality of opportunity in principle, but only 55 per cent favoured the adoption of positive discrimination as a means of achieving this goal. A fifth of the sample sat on the fence, undecided about whether this was a legitimate strategy or not.

On specific social issues, 85 per cent favoured the abolition of eleven-plus selection for secondary schools and the introduction of comprehensive education – one of the major political issues of that time. Considerably fewer (54 per cent) supported the more radical step of abolishing streaming in schools; but nearly two-thirds of the sample was strongly against prescription charges and private medical schemes – an issue which aroused considerable feelings at the time.

On industrial policies, hotly debated in the sixties and seventies, 71 per cent favoured an extension of public ownership and industrial democracy: 43 per cent supporting the more radical notion of workers' control as the ultimate objective of industrial relations policies. This was, of course, a fundamentally anti-capitalist stance, although whether all its supporters understood it as such is perhaps doubtful.

There was similarly widespread support (over 60 per cent) for the immediate abandonment of British nuclear weapons as a first step towards general nuclear disarmament, reflecting the wide CND/peace movement involvement noted earlier. But only about two-fifths of the sample agreed with the proposition that Britain should withdraw from NATO and adopt a positive neutralist foreign policy. Indeed, on what might be regarded as the three hard-left issues (abolition of streaming in schools, workers' control of industry and withdrawal from NATO), support was down to 53.6, 43.4 and 42.7 per cent respectively, and strong

Table 1.7 Contemporary attitude to key political and social issues of the 1960s and 70s

Percentage agreement/disagreement

	1	2	3	4	5 †
Class division was a major characteristic of British society	3.5	3.5	8.2	16.5	68.2
Racial divisions were a major problem in British society	3.6	8.4	14.5	30.1	43.4
Male chauvinism or dominance was a major problem in British society	4.8	13.1	35.7	26.2	20.2
Positive discrimination was a legitimate form of social engineering, to be adopted in appropriate situations	11.6	12.8	20.9	29.1	25.6
Social policy should be based on the notion of equality of opportunity	0.0	0.0	4.7	14.1	81.2
The 11+ should be abolished and grammar and secondary modern schools replaced by comprehensive schools	9.2	2.3	3.4	14.9	70.1
Streaming should be abolished in schools	17.9	14.3	14.3	14.3	39.3
NHS charges and private medical schemes should be abolished	5.9	12.9	14.1	2.4	64.7
Public ownership should be extended and industrial democracy increased	6.3	10.1	12.7	16.5	54.4
Workers' control should be the ultimate objective of all industrial relations and policies	18.1	25.3	13.3	14.5	28.9
British nuclear weapons should be abandoned immediately as a step towards general nuclear disarmament	17.4	14.0	7.0	17.4	44.2
Britain should withdraw from NATO and adopt a positive neutralist foreign policy	31.7	15.9	9.8	13.4	29.3

agreement was only 39.3, 28.9 and 29.3 per cent. That was the measure of the real support for the left-of-Labour 'protest and change' culture.

Respondents were also invited to indicate their agreement or disagreement with the same policies or views today. Some of the modifications no doubt reflect the process of ageing, but others perhaps the change in the political climate since the sixties and seventies. After a decade of Thatcher/Major 'classless' ideology, 10 per cent less now agree strongly that Britain is a class-divided society but (depressingly), 13 per cent more feel strongly that racial divisions are a major problem. Far fewer (12 per cent rather than 36 per cent) now sit on the fence about male chauvinism: 71 per cent agree that male chauvinism is a major problem in British society today, as opposed to 46 per cent in the earlier period.

Less of the sample also now sits on the fence over positive discrimination: 10 per cent more now favour such a strategy. Unsurprisingly, the attitude to equality of opportunity has changed very little – most people still being in favour.

The eleven-plus and comprehensive education are rather less of an issue than they were in the sixties and seventies, and this possibly explains why 14 per cent fewer expressed strong support for the abolition of selective education now. There has been a noticeable drift towards more mild support or a neutral position on this issue, reflecting a greater degree of uncertainty than there was 25 years ago. There is similarly greater uncertainty now about the abolition of streaming in schools: indeed there has been a quite clear shift of about 12 per cent from opposition to support for streaming.

There have been similar modifications of other 'progressive' or left-wing attitudes. Twelve per cent fewer now strongly disapprove of NHS charges and private medicine – they now only mildly disapprove.

---

† Key to Table 1.7

1 = strong disagreement
2 = mild disagreement
3 = neutral/disagreement
4 = mild agreement
5 = strong agreement

Fourteen per cent fewer agree with the extension of public owner-ship and industrial democracy and opposition to workers' control has increased by 24 per cent. There have been rather smaller shifts away from strong support for, to mild disapproval of, nuclear disarmament (4 per cent) and for withdrawal from NATO (6 per cent).

So far it has been shown that to a very considerable extent the 87 adult educators in this sample had risen (or felt they had risen) out of their working class or lower-middle class origins into the ranks of the middle class by virtue of their education (either as successful eleven-plus entrants to selective grammar schools or by taking the private school route to educational privilege) and/or by their professionalisation. Their loyalties and their political views were shaped more by their education than by their class origins. They had a strong inclination towards an intellectual culture which combined social criticism, scepticism and anti-establishment protest, with a tinge of revolutionary thinking. They were overwhelmingly *Guardian* and *Observer* readers with an interest in a wide range of radical and alternative journals. Their political culture was a mixture of optimism about the future; an expectation that the world could and should be changed for the better; and strong objection if the Establishment appeared to be hindering this progress. Ideologically they were predominantly Labourist or social democratic but with a sizeable minority to the left of Labour. They were extremely active politically, both in the mainstream political and trade union structures, but also in the sixties protest movements. They were very much in favour of peace and nuclear disarmament; a strengthened national health service; wor-kers' control in industry; comprehensive schools; and equality of oppor-tunity everywhere. They were against racism, apartheid, the Vietnam War and human exploitation and injustice wherever it was to be found.

The extent to which these young recruits to adult education in the later sixties and early seventies believed that adult education could contribute to the process of changing society for the better, and how it affected their professional practice, will be examined in Part 2.

part two

The Influence of the Sixties Culture on Adult Education

Reasons for Involvement in Adult Education

In the 1961–2 survey the majority of part-time tutors had regarded the need to earn money or the wish to teach their subject to adults as the main reasons for their involvement in adult education. Only a small number mentioned a sense of the social importance of their work. But amongst full-time tutors, a 'social philosophy' was the commonest reason, mentioned more frequently than the wish to teach adults. [32] Three main outcomes to adult education were regarded as of roughly equal importance: learning a subject (the content); the development of the individual students; and the social effect, or social purpose. [33]

Ruddock concluded that for many adult education tutors at that time 'their social-political value systems are of high personal importance. This is probably the most significant aspect for adult education of a tutor's political commitment; it gives him [sic] the reassurance that his [sic] work meets an urgent social need ...' [34] But interestingly Ruddock seems to have identified some loss of the original social purpose commitment by the early sixties. He noted that amongst the youngest age-groups, tutors were 'more academically inclined, less socially involved, more confused about their role as adult educationalists, looking more towards internal appointments ... (and) regard academic attainment as the means of advance.' [35]

This precise point was echoed by one of those interviewed in the current survey when he recalled that 'many people in the field were concerned to ensure their academic respectability and credibility as opposed to the earlier sense of social purpose which predecessors had'. A similar attitude was demonstrated by another of the current sample. As a mature student, he really wanted to obtain a job in higher education and joined the WEA very much as a stepping stone. He had no previous knowledge of adult education, but 'stumbled into it'. Many others likewise came into adult education largely by accident rather than with any strong sense of commitment. For them it was 'just a job' or better than 'going round on a wheel' week-by-week in industry. But the initial 'accident' often led to enthusiasm:

> *I fell into adult education completely by accident. I used to go to the odd class myself as consumer, and I was looking for ways of earning small bits of money to eke out my (research) grant ... It wasn't a strong sense of social purpose. I love teaching ... but I don't like young children. So I just found my niche.*

The pleasures of teaching were not always so accidentally discovered: they were what attracted some to adult education. Sometimes it did not matter very much whether it was teaching in schools or with adults. But for others, it was the adult dimension that was the attraction, such as the Cambridge research fellow who came across a number of mature students studying for their education degree. This drew his attention 'to the notion of how interesting it might be to work with people who were older'. When he started applying for adult education jobs 'there was a push and a pull element' which illustrated the varied and sometimes contradictory forces which attracted people to adult education:

> *I was predisposed to it: I did have a definite strong feeling that that was what I wanted to do and that I wanted to work with older people .... But secondly there was a strong compulsion aspect – giving up research, giving up writing. I'm not going to spend my time in the ivory tower, I'm not going to work with privileged undergraduates ... It wasn't just reaction ... but there was that element of guilt.*

That element of guilt was half-way to the social conscience which did lead many to adult education in the sixties and seventies. With some it 'chimed in with vague feelings' that they 'ought to be doing something which was mildly socially purposeful'. For others it was a 'very strong belief that adult education would help to achieve a changed society'. As one university tutor expressed it: 'I was hoping to achieve social and political change' through teaching. A WEA appointee in the late sixties was 'attracted to the WEA by the notion of being able to make a significant contribution to the education of the working class' (even if 'the WEA turned out to be not quite the radical organisation one hoped for'). He was responding to the 'strong motivation in the mid-sixties towards work directly with and on behalf of the working class'. Similarly an ex-Ruskin student recalls:

> *From my time at Ruskin my aim was to go back and bring what I had back to (the working class) ... I thought it would make a difference. (Therefore) when I was looking for jobs, it was in adult education I was looking for them.*

'Firmly held political and social beliefs about the importance of education in terms of a broad political context' were in fact a strong attraction for some of those coming into adult education at that time. It could be 'as a process of informing':

> *I never thought of adult education as something one went into as a profession ... It was done on the basis of a strong political and social commitment ... Not with the intention or any thought that it was one's contribution to fundamentally changing the world. But changing the world was an important part of it ... Changing it by informing people.*

For others on the left, the political goals were a more conscious intention. For one WEA tutor, coming straight from the world of student politics and the hothouse of New Left Marxist theory:

> *Coming into the WEA was a way of achieving political change rather than being a commitment to adult education ... The WEA was a place to come and be political ... Political change would come as a result of lots of us doing this kind of thing ... I saw us as being in the vanguard of the cultural struggle (by teaching*

*workers and the professional proletariat) ... We were getting
ourselves into positions of influence ... I did believe there was a
genuine chance of a different social order ... (Adult education
would) create radical and political consciousness.*

He believed that by enabling the working class leaders to challenge
the hegemonic ideas and to understand the Marxist alternatives, political
consciousness would filter down to the workers. 'Putting Marxism on
the agenda and demystifying bourgeois ideology and raising a substantial
critique of bourgeois culture' in the footsteps of Edward Thompson and
Raymond Williams was thus the attraction and purpose of adult education for some of the sixties generation.

However, it is very clear that both the degree and nature of the social
or political commitment and sense of purpose brought by the new recruits
into this world of adult education in the late sixties and early seventies
varied enormously, as did the extent to which they were ever conscious
of such commitment. The distinction between ideological indoctrination
or party political propaganda and the role of education was clearly
understood, but within the context of education there were quite widely
differing emphases.

A Spectrum of Social Purpose

At one end of the spectrum were straightforward views that 'transfor-
ming the political arena' was simply not on the agenda, at least for
government-funded adult education; or that adult education should not
be used 'deliberately as a platform'. But in reality, even without such
deliberate intent, there is no absolute divide between education and
political effect. As the comment of an ex-WEA development officer
makes clear:

*I think adult education should be used as a vehicle for promoting
social change. What it must not do is provide propaganda on one
side of the political line or the other ... I do believe that as a*

process of adult education, if one is then stimulated to carry a banner in favour of CND or the Labour Party or any of these things, that is a legitimate end-product of adult education, but it's secondary – it's not the primary aim ...

What was widely – perhaps universally – accepted was the distinction between political neutrality (identified by one WEA tutor as a 'bourgeois myth') and objectivity ('endeavouring to look at all sides of the argument'), which one strived for. It was therefore unacceptable to be 'pushing any one particular line except the line that (the students) had abilities'. This confidence-building was the legitimate aim. As one tutor expressed it, 'the aim was to stimulate people intellectually' so that they were 'taken out of themselves and made to realise that they've got capabilities ... which can be used'.

This largely passive but significant social role for adult education was emphasised by a number of respondents:

Adult education ... gave people a chance to branch out from where they were either into political activity, whatever it happened to be, or just into expressing themselves more – having a more satisfactory life through being able to do things that it wouldn't necessarily have occurred to them to do ... I wasn't trying to promote any particular party line through adult education ... I just actually believed from my own experience that education ... is (a) satisfactory in itself and (b) it opens your mind to other things and (c) it gives you possibilities to do other things in your life.

Part of trying to promote a public understanding of science is to do with enfranchising people and enabling them to take part in discussions and therefore to make sensible decisions about how science and technology affects their lives and whether they want to control and influence it in any way. But it wasn't my purpose to suggest that for them and I didn't have that uppermost in my mind ... It is not for us to promote particular purposes ... I didn't see myself there as an agent for social change other than being an agent for education, which might in turn of course lead to social change ... I just felt that the more people who had access to the world of ideas for whatever purpose, the better ... My agenda was mainly an intellectual one rather than a social one in so far as you can separate those, although you can't separate them.

I was very committed to the idea that people should know and understand more about their natural environment, and that they should have access to the practical skills and theoretical background to conservation.

This passive or apparently 'neutral' approach sometimes revealed itself as being less neutral than its exponents realised. Whether the hope was to promote conservation or, as another stated, a 'more harmonious, fairer, more tolerant society', these were not neutral objectives (however desirable they might be). This was more clearly recognised by another interviewee who suggested that:

... by trying to develop that elusive commodity, rationality, in a much more effective way ... other people might see the same things as you do but you don't have to tell them the way in which to change the world. If they have a greater understanding of the world they will be with you changing it in the direction you're interested in.

This lies at the heart of how so many people really felt about adult education. It was not a medium of propaganda: it was a means of extending understanding and rationality and building confidence. But the result would be a better world: a world changing in the direction they believed to be desirable. For example, a better understanding of the world would result in more effective democratic processes. This was not regarded by those who advocated it as radical social change so much as a liberal humanist approach which would help to produce 'a radical informed consciousness in a modern democracy'. Adult education's role was thus to provide 'social information', empowering individuals, enabling them to challenge the establishment, and 'undermine the over-respect for institutions'. One respondent recalled that he 'believed that the injustices of society could be alleviated by raising awareness and empowering the disadvantaged. ... I felt that adult education had a part to play in this'. Others suggested that adult education specifically helped women 'to come to understand their own situation better and to empower themselves'. Imperceptibly the intention had moved from merely providing access to knowledge, to something a little more active. 'What we were trying to do was teach (people) the ways of combating what seemed to be happening to them'. However, this was not regarded as political action: 'it seemed just intensely, positively right'.

One interviewee, a sociologist, stated that she was 'interested in effecting social change, and in questions of equality and justice and redistributing resources and access and making sure that people who didn't have chances the first time round got them the second time round'. However, the task was so enormous that it was inevitable, she thought, that all adult education could do was help some people to improve their position, rather than instigate general social change. This was echoed by another tutor when he said:

One knows one can't shift mountains ... In teaching I've always been wanting to help the individual who wanted to get on ... In teaching adults you hope that some of them ... use it as a stepping stone and you hope you can help these at least to see where the next steps are.

Thus adult education was widely regarded as a mixture of confidence-building, the extension of rationality and understanding, access to useful knowledge and social information, raising awareness, empowering individuals and providing stepping stones or opportunities for individuals to take. Sometimes the emphasis was on individual development and fulfilment, sometimes on collective social action. But there was no fundamental conflict in this dichotomy, as one interviewee explained:

I don't see ... any real conflict between the individual goals and

> *the collective goals ... (because) the aggregate of individual*
> *growth is going to be an enrichment of society and communal life.*

A similar point was made by another interviewee who saw his role as both 'changing the world' and 'helping any individual within this present rotten world to get into the pleasure of learning ... and to be able to make the move from grubby manual labour ... I don't see any incompatibility between the two'.

A metaphor that was applied quite frequently to adult education was that it provided students with tools which they could then use for various purposes – either individual or collective. But as one tutor remarked, there was possibly a distinction to be drawn between tools and weapons. She saw education as giving people tools but without any control over what they should do with them:

> *You just happen to believe that people are better off with tools*
> *than without them ... What you're giving them are tools rather*
> *than weapons. I think most of the things you give people can only*
> *be used in a creative way...*

But there are, of course, many different ways of being creative, and not everyone agrees about what is desirably creative. The tutor just quoted (who believed that adult education would create a more harmonious society) may not have agreed totally with the one who explained that the task was firstly to provide politically relevant information (the evidence) and then to teach students how to interpret and handle that evidence, hoping that they would then be able to analyse the social and political situation for themselves. These were altogether more politically-tuned tools (or weapons). Some politically committed tutors undoubtedly did over-step the bounds of objectivity, as one recalls:

> *There was a bit of Gradgrindery about the lefties of the sixties:*
> *there were the little vessels waiting to be filled. All I've got to do is*
> *come along – the ideologue who knows it all – and tell them ... It*
> *was youthful enthusiasm and naivety – but it's an arrogance of*

32

*sorts as well ... What I was looking for in the sixties was
conversion ... It was a quasi-religious fervour that we had.*

But more typical was the equally left-wing tutor who quite clearly
drew the distinction between providing students with information and
analytical tools (both legitimate) and direct political action or advocacy.
As a teacher he always believed in the old anarchist notion that people
will use education in the most useful ways. Therefore although teaching
is clearly a political activity, and the teacher is a consciousness-raiser,
ultimately people should be left to their own devices as to what they do
with the information and the tools one gives them, even though one might
hope that they use them in a particular way.

It is that hope that adult education will change attitudes and therefore
lead to social and political change, while at the same time trying to adopt
an objective pedagogical approach, that typifies many of the adult
educators of the sixties era. But of course there were many variants within
this overall model. Not least, as one interviewee explained, 'there was
quite a strong ideological divergence between the people who viewed
themselves basically as adult educationists and the people who viewed
themselves as subject specialists'. The latter were likely to be more
committed to their discipline and less to the social and political purposes
of adult education.

There were also very considerable differences between the university departments up and down the country; with differences in ethos.
They attracted different kinds of staff: some would emphasise subject
specialisms, others the social purpose of adult education. At one university, where academic excellence and integration within the university
were primary objectives, it is recalled that with the majority of staff 'their
first loyalty was to their subject'. Other universities were quite different.

The Balance of Priorities

The responses of the adult educators in the current questionnaire survey
suggest that promoting social and political change through adult educa-

tion was generally considered of less importance or legitimacy than teaching, organising or research in tutors' subject specialisms. Table 2.1 illustrates the relative weighting attributed by the sample to six different aspects of adult education work. [36]

Table 2.1 Adult Education Priorities

	Relative weighting based on 85 responses	
	When they started AE	*Now*
Teaching	25.3	23.3
Developing new areas of AE	17.9	19.7
Organising AE programmes	17.2	18.2
Study and research in particular subject/disciplines	16.8	12.3
Achieving social/political change through AE	14.4	13.7
Study and research in the field of adult continuing education	8.4	12.8
Total	**100.00**	**100.00**

There has been surprisingly little change in the order of priorities between the period when the respondents started work in adult education in the sixties and seventies, and the present day, except that research in the field of adult continuing education has become somewhat more important at the expense of subject-oriented research.

A slightly different order of priorities emerges when the most important activity only is taken into account (although this does not change the picture significantly). Forty-five per cent of the respondents put teaching as their highest priority, or joint top priority, in the sixties and seventies. This was way above any other activity. Seventeen per cent considered research in their subject specialism to be their first (or joint first) priority, followed by organising an adult education programme (13.8 per cent), developing new areas of adult education (11.6 per cent), and then promoting social and political change through adult education

(11.0 per cent). Only one person stated that research in the field of adult continuing education was the highest priority.

This corresponds closely with the finding of the 1961–2 survey which concluded that the majority of tutors then preferred teaching, although 'about one-third found teaching and organising to be equally appealing'.[37] The conditions in which most tutors worked left very little opportunity for research after the essential duties of teaching and organising had been carried out, so research inevitably became a lesser priority.[38]

As indicated above, only 11 per cent of the present sample regarded the promotion of social and political change through adult education as their top priority, but this is perhaps to be expected, given that adult educationalists were paid to teach, organise and sometimes undertake research.

Moreover, as one interviewee suggested, conditions did not altogether favour those who, like himself, would have liked the work to be more socially purposeful. It was not practical because '90 per cent of the people who belonged to the WEA were seeking ... personal enrichment (which) ... added to the quality of their life'. This was perfectly legitimate, but they did not see themselves as part of 'a movement for social change'. Therefore all he could do as a development officer was act pragmatically by concentrating on organising classes which met the wishes of this student body, rather than trying to ferment social change.

If, therefore, there was only a small minority who openly regarded adult education as a means of pursuing what they considered to be the more important political goal of reforming society, there were a considerable number of others who regarded social/political change as a perfectly legitimate, even desirable, by-product and therefore did not place it at the bottom of their list of priorities. (Indeed, less than one-third of the respondents put social/political change as the least important objective.)

The Spectrum of Social Purpose Re-visited

When asked more specifically whether they agreed or disagreed with certain political or social purposes of adult education at the time when they began work in adult education, nearly everyone (95.5 per cent) agreed that it should enrich students' lives and enable them to better fulfil their individual potential, and more than three-quarters also agreed that adult education should provide knowledge which then became the individual students' own 'property' to use as they saw fit. Thus a vast majority saw adult education as contributing to the growth and development of the individuals whom they taught. Significantly fewer respondents (43.6 per cent) felt that adult education should enable individuals to improve their position in society. A considerable number (nearly one-third of the total) expressed no opinion one way or the other about this proposition, and a quarter disagreed with it, reflecting the traditional British view of liberal adult education – that it should be 'for its own sake' rather than for any material purpose.

Two-thirds of the respondents agreed with the suggestion that adult education should help to create a more egalitarian society, and over half supported the rather stronger propositions that it should empower students to take social and political action, or that it should positively discriminate in favour of the working class or other specific disadvantaged groups, to enable them to be more effective in their struggles for a better or juster society. But, somewhat surprisingly, rather fewer respondents (41 per cent) felt that adult education should have helped students to become more community-oriented and involved in community politics. (A third of the respondents expressed no opinion on this proposition, perhaps reflecting a certain lack of understanding of its exact meaning.)

The most radical and contentious proposition, reflecting some of the historic aims of the British adult education movement, that it should become the educational arm of political forces in their struggle for a more just society, attracted support from only one-fifth of the respondents, while three-fifths disagreed with this objective. The responses are sum-

Table 2.2 Political/Social purpose of adult education

Adult education should:	Strongly disagree %	Disagree %	Neutral %	Agree %	Strongly agree %
1. Enable people to enrich their lives and better fulfil their own personal potential	01.1	01.1	02.3	24.1	71.3
2. Enable individuals to improve their position in society	09.4	15.3	31.8	31.8	11.8
3. Provide knowledge which was then the individual student's property to use as s/he wished	04.8	02.4	16.7	39.3	36.9
4. Help to create a more egalitarian society	08.1	09.3	17.4	33.7	31.4
5. Help people to become community-oriented and involved in community politics	13.3	13.3	32.5	24.1	16.9
6. Empower people to take social and political action	14.0	09.3	24.4	23.3	29.1
7. Positively discriminate in favour of working class or other specific disadvantaged groups, to enable them to be more effective in their struggle for a better or juster society	18.8	10.6	20.0	21.2	29.4
8. Become the educational arm of political forces in their struggle for a more just society	40.7	19.8	18.6	09.3	11.6

marised in Table 2.2. When the respondents are divided into left, centre and right-wing politically, some interesting variations in attitudes emerge. [39] For example, whereas 78.8 per cent of the centre and right-wing respondents strongly agreed that adult education should enable individuals to enrich their lives and better fulfil their individual potential, less than half the left-wingers strongly agreed with this. Similarly, 100 per cent of the right-wingers and 78.6 per cent of the centrists agreed that the knowledge acquired by students in adult education classes was their own 'property' to use as they wished, but only 58 per cent of the left-wingers felt this. There was considerably less support for adult education as an individualistic or private activity amongst left-wingers.

Conversely, they supported adult education as a collectivist activity more strongly. Two-thirds of the left group strongly agreed that adult education should help create a more egalitarian society, but less than a quarter of the centre and none of the right strongly agreed: indeed 44 per cent of the right disagreed. Similarly, three-quarters of the left were in favour of adult education contributing to community politics, but only 31.5 per cent of the centre and 22 per cent of the right agreed (and two-thirds of the right disagreed).

Almost all those on the left (95 per cent) felt that adult education should empower people to take social and political action and that it should positively discriminate in favour of the working class or other specific disadvantaged groups, to help them in their struggle for a better or more just society, but only some 43 per cent of the centre agreed. None of the right agreed that adult education should empower people but one right-winger did support positive discrimination.

On the most radical and contentious proposition, that adult education should become the educational arm of political forces for change, over half the left agreed, but 70 per cent of the centre and 100 per cent of the right disagreed (indeed all the right strongly disagreed).

When asked to state in their own words what they considered to be the most important aim(s) or purpose(s) for adult education when they first started work, over half the respondents reiterated that enabling individuals to fulfil themselves and develop their potential or enrich their lives was the most important purpose. And when asked which of the purposes listed in Table 2.2 had been most effectively achieved over the past 20–25 years, 84 per cent believed it was the enrichment and personal development of individuals. Nothing else was regarded as having been a significant achievement except the provision of knowledge which individuals could use as they wished (6.7 per cent).

This predominantly individualist perspective is reflected in other responses to the invitation to state the most important aims and purposes for adult education. Sixteen people mentioned the provision of a second chance or greater access to educational opportunities. In addition, 'giving the educationally disadvantaged opportunities and the pleasure of education' and 'providing a route to escape from rotten jobs' were both mentioned. Providing an opportunity for individuals to improve their position in society was mentioned five times and opportunities to increase knowledge 12 times. Other individualistic reasons mentioned between one and three times included:

- to share my enthusiasm for knowledge and understanding of the world around us (1)
- promote better understanding of a subject (1)
- arouse curiosity (1)
- encourage people to think for themselves (1)
- popularise culture (2)
- develop social awareness and extend intellectual horizons (1)
- entertainment (1)
- social intercourse (1)
- develop a better understanding of the individual's part in the social context (1)
- raise awareness of different cultural traditions (3)
- increase tolerance (2)
- enable individuals to contribute more effectively to society (1).

Towards the end of the above list of write-in responses, there is a swing towards less individualist, more social purposes. Other responses which reflected the belief that adult education could and should contribute towards collective social change rather than merely the improvement of individuals included:

- empowering people to take social or political action (10)
- help disadvantaged groups to attain greater social justice and equality (8)
- create a more egalitarian society (6)
- create a more just and critical society (1)
- create a more educated and better society (1)
- raise political consciousness (1)
- promote a better understanding of society – to enable people to change that society (1)
- produce a better informed, more caring society (1)
- enable individuals to arrive at a more informed judgement about issues effecting society and thereby participate more effectively in the decision-making processes (1)
- furthering collective interests and action (2)
- equip members of the working class to provide political leadership (1)
- train trade union representatives (1)
- improve the knowledge and understanding of the working class – to enable them to work for a more equitable society (1)
- enable working class people to understand and resist cultural hegemony and to rescue the progressive elements from bourgeois culture and use them for a proletarian order (1)
- promote social change (1).

Finally there were a few miscellaneous or specialist 'aims':

- to develop social-work skills (1)
- complete a research project on prison governor training (1)
- fulfil frustrated academic need (1)
- couldn't get a 'real' university job (1).

Attitudes to the Russell Report

The Russell Report, published in 1973, is now sometimes regarded somewhat nostalgically as a promise of a new future for British adult education which, for various reasons (mainly political), never materialised. For the universities, the Report envisaged 'a unique contribution ... to a fully comprehensive service of adult education,' more directly within the public system of education than it had been in the past. This meant concentrating specifically on work of university quality, or 'intellectual education', which the Report recognised would always be a minority concern – but one which was expected to 'enlarge rapidly' over the next decade. [40]

The implication was that the universities should pull back from too great an involvement in low-level adult education, but in practice the Report's recommendations for the universities involved little change. It proposed that the universities should concentrate on:

1. liberal studies of the traditional kind, characterised by intellectual effort by the students

2. 'balancing' (or conversion) continuing education

3. role education for groups whose common element was their role in society

4. industrial education at all levels, from management to the shop floor

5. project research work

6. training for those engaged in the education of adults and research in adult education as an academic discipline.[41]

None of this would necessarily have involved the universities in changing their activities very much. More radical was the recommendation that they could also undertake more elementary pioneer work 'to open up the cultivation of new fields which, once cultivated, could be handed over to other agencies'. [42] This pioneer work would include courses in new fields for professional and vocational groups; work for disadvantaged groups; and provision for adult access to higher education and other qualifications at an advanced level. The report saw 'a mounting need here' and expressed the hope that the universities would 'explore this field energetically'. [43]

Organisationally, the Report gave support to existing specialist extra-mural or adult education departments, but also to those universities which wished to integrate adult education more closely with their day-to-day teaching and research. [44]

For the WEA, the Report concluded that 'the roles of the WEA as both promoter of adult education for the universities (and other bodies) and provider of its own programme of classes should continue', but nudged it quite definitely towards 'a shift of emphasis from a wide range of general provision to more specific priorities', leaving some of its previous functions to other providing bodies. The 'specific priorities' consisted of four areas which the WEA itself had identified as its special interest, and which became known as the WEA's 'Russell-type work'. They were:

1. education for the socially and culturally deprived living in urban areas – of an experimental and informal character

2. work in an industrial context (predominantly trade union education)

3. developing greater social and political awareness (which the Report considered to be of 'special value')

4. liberal and academic study below the level of university work.

In the last category, it was envisaged that the WEA would move gradually to a more promotional role for other bodies rather than making direct provision itself, and that there would inevitably be a weakening of the links with the universities in providing joint courses. All-in-all, the Report argued that this shift in emphasis would 'once again cast the WEA largely in the role of educational pioneer'. [45]

The Report recommended an increase in public expenditure on adult education over a five- to seven-year period from about £17.4m to

£40.65m. Most of this was LEA expenditure, with the DES share being £1.25m rising to £2.65m. [46] The Report's recommendations also required an enhanced contribution from the universities, and the UGC was encouraged to recognise this. [47]

Some of the tutors and lecturers who had come into adult education shortly before the publication of the Russell Report did regard it as an opportunity for the adult education movement to get back to its more radical roots. It seemed to reflect, and indeed encourage, the political radicalism of the sixties culture. 'It did hold out the chance for, if not a wholesale change of direction, a change of emphasis ... It was certainly talking about disadvantage ... It was a watershed of opportunity'. It 'gave us a platform from which to change the very conservative nature of the WEA' – particularly to concentrate on disadvantaged groups and to bring a more politically social purpose dimension to the work. It is remembered by some as an exciting opportunity (even if many others now find it quite difficult to remember anything very much about the content of the Report).

Those less radical in their politics or their expectation of adult education, recollect it as being altogether less significant:

> *It certainly wasn't a watershed.*
> *I don't remember it having any major impact.*
> *I thought it is full of good intentions but doesn't really go forward.*
> *It got lost in its own verbiage. It recommended a bit more of the same with a slight tinkering of the edges ...*
> *It made adult education look rather safe, rather boring and not worth putting any investment into ...*
> *It didn't ask sharp questions ... I don't think it put a strong enough case ... Somehow you felt it was tired.*

The questionnaire invited respondents to choose one of four value judgements about the Russell Report, reflecting most accurately their assessment of it at the time, and their view of it today. Table 2.3 summarises the 61 responses to this question, sub-divided into the same left, centre and right-wing groups as earlier. [48]

Table 2.3 Reaction to the Russell Report

	In 1973			1973	Today
	Left	Centre	Right	All %	All %
	Number of responses				
It was a reactionary report, attempting to divert adult education into more utilitarian directions, diluting its traditional social purpose	–	–	1	1.6	3.1
It was a wishy-washy report which missed a real opportunity to re-direct adult education towards more exciting and worth-while goals because it was too moderate in its funding demands and really recommended a 'bit more of the same'	10	5	3	29.5	26.6
It was a useful/interesting report but largely irrelevant because it depended on a significant increase in funding which everyone knew would not be forthcoming	3	27	1	50.8	64.1
It was a watershed, which enabled adult education to find its way again, particularly by concentrating effort and resources on specific targets and advocating positive discrimination for disadvantaged groups, and thus legitimated socially committed political work	6	5	–	18.0	6.3
Total	**19**	**37**	**5**	**100.00**	**100.00**

Overall there was a tendency to regard the Report as useful and interesting but largely irrelevant because there were no funds to support its recommendations. This view has grown from 50 per cent to two-thirds of the sample, when looking back from today's vantage point. But this was not so much the view of the left-wingers, who, as already mentioned, were more inclined to regard the Report as an opportunity to re-direct adult education towards more worthwhile goals or as a significant watershed which did help adult education to find its way again, particularly by concentrating on more socially committed, political work. Or they regarded it as a missed opportunity to recapture this social purpose. If implemented, it could have been a new stage. 'It seemed significant at the time, but I'm not sure it ever was. It caused a stir but not an impact ... It didn't effect our working practices'. It was seen as having failed to change the culture towards effective lifelong education. If it was a watershed of opportunity, 'now I see it as a watershed of missed opportunity'.

Partly its progressive aims were hampered by a lack of resources. The extra funding envisaged by Russell was not forthcoming. But its effectiveness was also undermined by the lack of will within the voluntary movements:

> *If we tried to apply (the Russell priorities) to the WEA, then half the members would run away ... They were terrified of things like social and political (purpose) and the unemployed.*

A judgement which perhaps best sums up the collective recollection of the Russell Report's impact was that a great deal of hope was attached to it, but it became more of a millstone than a watershed.

If the non-implementation of the Russell Report represents a failure to invest adult education with the progressive radicalism of the sixties culture, this was also inhibited to some extent by a divergence of views between the newly-appointed young adult educators and their employers.

Constraints on Radical Social Purpose

Nearly two-fifths of the current sample claimed that there was some tension between their aims and aspirations and those of their first employer in adult education. Sometimes this was a purely personal tension between people who did not get on very well, but at other times it was a clash of cultures or values. The most frequent cause of disagreement was the new tutors' wish to concentrate their efforts on meeting the needs of specific underprivileged groups as advocated by Russell, while the employer was more concerned with recruiting as many students as possible, whoever they were, in order to reach target numbers (mentioned 10 times). A similar problem occurred when tutors felt that their concern for educational quality was undermined by an employer whose only real concern was the quantity of enrolments (mentioned seven times).

Six respondents felt quite specifically that their attempts to promote adult education for political or social action had been thwarted by more cautious employers. Conversely, two respondents felt they came under pressure to promote political or social aims whereas they merely wanted to 'get on with their job'. One or two people also experienced tensions over having to follow fixed syllabuses; having to put too much emphasis on training or adopt a particular approach to a subject, or methodological differences.

Another common cause of tension or disagreement was the tutor feeling inhibited from implementing new ideas or promoting certain aims or aspirations by a hierarchical organisation (mentioned nine times) or by internal managerial constraints (19 times).

All these constraints were much more likely to be experienced within the WEA than the universities, where, as one interviewee explained, 'you were very much on your own'. And within the WEA they were much more likely to come from the voluntary movement than from the District Secretaries, who generally 'tended to be progressive'. This has already been noted in connection with the Russell Report. One tutor specifically recalls that the voluntary movement was dominated by a majority who were conservatively opposed to the Russell priorities. Another recalls the hostility to trade union work. The tutor-organisers saw it as their job to 'nurse the voluntary movement' through the necessary changes. This brought tensions and resistance.

Another tutor recalls that his District Committee had a very narrow view of what was desirable, based on a managerial interpretation of its role which lost sight of 'how socially useful something might be'. Another recollection (from one of the most conservative respondents in the survey) was that 'the WEA was a peculiar mix of autocracy and well-meaning inefficiency ... The collectivist front of democracy actually hid one of the two most illiberal sets of practices I've ever come across' leading to what he describes as 'a sort of tyranny'.

The funding bodies or 'the paymasters' were regarded as something of a constraint by 28 respondents. The main problem was the rather restricted or limited interpretation of what was permissible under the Government's further education regulations. But interestingly, the HM Inspectorate was largely exonerated from any blame in this.

Other causes of constraint were the general political climate (mentioned eight times), peer group pressure (six times), the unreadiness of the students for radical change, or personal factors – 'your own inadequacies or your own lack of capacity'. A sense of disillusionment was referred to seven times and a realisation that their aims were unrealistic, eight times. 'Some of the dreams that some of us may have had in the sixties about radical interventions via education ... were somewhat utopian'.

As one of the more left-wing respondents put it, they did believe that socialism could be built in a reasonable time and that adult education would help by 'maturing the counter-culture into a fully-fledged political opposition' and 'creating a genuinely extended working class culture with socialist intellectuals'. But unfortunately for such aspirations:

history wasn't on our side ... We were at the end of a period of activism rather than at the beginning of the long struggle ... What was wrong was that we had too facile an expectation of changing consciousness. It doesn't work like that. It's a much larger process

than that – creating a culture. We hadn't spent enough time
thinking about what was the nature of that culture that we were
trying to create.

In general, the majority of tutors did not feel particularly restricted or constrained in pursuing their objectives for adult education, but clearly a sizeable minority did feel so constrained, either by their employers or external forces or the general political climate or by internal constraints – a personal sense of disillusionment or a feeling that their aims had been unrealistic.

The Influence of the Sixties Culture on Adult Education in the Universities and the WEA

What, then, happened to the optimism and joyful irreverence? This survey has shown that the 'sixties generation' of adult educators did bring their cultural baggage and their attitudes with them into the world of university and WEA adult education. They tended to be a socially mobile meritocracy, risen into the ranks of the middle class by virtue of their education and/or professionalisation. They were overwhelmingly *Guardian, Observer, New Statesman* readers and had imbibed the sixties radical intellectual culture. They tended to be centre-left (with a minority further to the left), politically active, anti-establishment protesters. They did believe the world could and should be changed for the better. Their reasons for coming into adult education were quite mixed and not always very clearly planned. Indeed there was often a strong accidental element.

What they expected to achieve in adult education varied very considerably, but a belief that it would (and did) help individuals to achieve their personal potential and live more fulfilled lives was certainly the predominant motive. However, this was not seen as being at variance with the social purpose which many also shared. A sense of social guilt or social conscience made many want to promote a social purpose through adult education. By providing knowledge and informing people, by extending understanding and rationality, by building confidence and by raising consciousness, it was felt that the students would be empowered to challenge authority, take on the Establishment, and work for a better world. Adult education would provide the intellectual tools (or weapons) for this process, although for some this was regarded not so much as the central purpose as a by-product of adult education.

The Russell Report of 1973 was welcomed by some as an expression of this social purpose dimension. It reflected the optimistic aims of the sixties culture and offered an opportunity for adult education to recapture its radical social purpose. But for the majority it seemed (or now seems) largely irrelevant – a missed opportunity.

In the pursuit of their optimistic, joyful, irreverent, challenging purpose, some tutors did come up against constraints by more pragmatic or conservative employing bodies or funding agencies, or found that they ran out of steam or discovered that their aims had been somewhat unrealistic. But there is not the same overwhelming sense of constraint that was experienced by a similar generation of optimistic adult educators in the late forties and early fifties, with the onset of the Cold War. [49]

Finally, what changes have occurred in the ideas and aspirations of the 'sixties' adult educators between their early days and now? We saw in Part 1 that they have swung as a cohort from centre-left to centre-right politically. Table 2.1 shows little change in the relative importance attached to teaching, development, organising, research and achieving social change through adult education. Table 2.3 shows that they have a less radical concept of the Russell Report today that they had 20 years ago. There has been a widespread loss of belief amongst the respondents not in the desirability but in the efficacy of adult education as a means of changing the world. As one expressed it, 'the difference between then and now is that then I believed it could make some difference: now I have no conception that anything I do will make the slightest bit of difference.' Another declares that he has become more contemplative, less active or aggressive. A third says she has come to realise that adult education:

> *wasn't really the effective diet to cure a lot of the sort of problems that we were coming up against ... I felt that we were scratching at*

the surface and arousing people's expectations ... (but) education
was not as empowering as I had thought that it was ... In fact,
except for the very special individual, what we were offering
wasn't going to make a very big difference to what they could do.

This partly reflects the widespread pessimism of the changed political climate in the eighties and nineties – the general depoliticisation of
life and the growth of selfishness and competitiveness at the expense of
a belief in a general, collective good.

However, as one respondent points out, if one's expectations in the
sixties and seventies were less grandiose, if one never did believe in the
utopian possibilities of social engineering, then there is less of a sense of
failure now. A similar 'realism' is expressed by another respondent when
he says 'I feel that the "individual personal development" priority (for
adult education) is not the apparently apolitical or complacent option that
it might have appeared to be in the early '70s'.

An ability to adapt to changing circumstances and see different ways
of reaching one's goals is perhaps the reason why quite a few respondents
claim very little change in their expectations of adult education. As one
expressed it, he brought the optimism of the sixties into adult education
with him, and he still carries it. Another sees his concentration on
research partly as 'a retreat into quietism' but also as 'another kind of
activism' – bringing ideas forward in a different way.

Perhaps most reassuring is the respondent who came into adult
education the same year as the Russell Report was published, and now
occupies a chair in adult education, who has changed against the general
trend, becoming 'more and more conscious of the educational and
cultural damage inflicted in the last 12 years' and therefore increasing
his belief in 'favouring the disadvantaged, and for empowerment through
knowledge and skills'. Thus the optimism and sense of social purpose of
the sixties culture has not completely evaporated in the intervening years.

References

1. R. Ruddock, 'One hundred and seventy tutors', *Adult Education*, vol. xxxv, no. 5 (1963), pp 313–34.

2. *ibid.*, p 330.

3. I wish to acknowledge the assistance of Sue Milward in processing the raw data from the questionnaires and Tom Steele for analysing the responses to the question about cultural interests and for conducting some of the interviews.

4. Ruddock, *op. cit.*, p 313.

5. The UFC did make a grant towards the cost of this research project as part of its recent policy of funding continuing education research. It had no influence on the implementation of the project, or the writing of this monograph. However, the author is the first to recognise that ultimately funding does have strings attached.

6. Ruddock, *op. cit.*, p 313.

7. A. Marwick, *British Society Since 1945* (Pelican, 1982), p 178.

8. *ibid.*, pp 173–5.

9. D. Childs, *Britain Since 1945*, 2nd edn (Methuen, 1984), p 207.

10. *ibid.*, pp 208–9.

11. R. Harris, *The Making of Neil Kinnock* (Faber, 1984), pp 40–41. While at University, before joining the WEA, Kinnock had been an active member of CND and organised anti-apartheid protests; *ibid.*, pp 37 and 42.

12. A. Howard, written for the British Association for Counselling 1988 Conference.

13. Central Statistical Office, *Social Trends*, no. 1 (HMSO, 1970), p 124. The figure quoted is for 1969.

14. *ibid.*, p 125.

15. *ibid.*

16. *ibid.*

17. The percentages add up to over 100 because several people had attended more than one type of secondary school.

18. Ruddock, *op. cit.*, p 314.

19. *ibid.*

20. *ibid.*

21. Ruddock, *op. cit.*, p 318.

22. The responses to this question on cultural interests were analysed by Tom Steele. I am very much indebted to him for the following analysis.

23. Ruddock, *op. cit.*, p 318.

24. R.L. Leonard, *Guide to the General Election* (Pan, 1964) pp 68–72; R. Taylor, 'To the Left of Labour: Revolutionary Politics in Britain 1920–1980', unpublished paper (1981).

25. Ruddock, *op. cit.*, p 318.

26. D. Coates, *The Context of British Politics* (Hutchinson, 1984), p 254.

27. Ruddock, *op. cit.*, pp 322–3.

28. Central Office of Information, Reference Pamphlet 97, 'The British Press', (HMSO, 1976) pp 6–9 and 13.

29. R. Williams, 'General Profile' in R. Hoggart (ed.), *Your Sunday Paper* (University of London Press, 1967), p 16.

30. Ruddock, *op. cit.*, p 323.

31. *ibid.*

32. *ibid.*, p 316.

33. *ibid.*, p 317.

34. *ibid.*, p 318.

35. *ibid.*, p 329

36. Respondents were invited to place the six activities in order of importance. Some respondents recorded equal importance for more than one activity,

rather than a simple rating of one to six. In Table 2.1 all the responses have been aggregated to show the relative overall importance attributed to each activity. The higher the percentage, the more important the activity was regarded by the sample as a whole.

37. Ruddock, *op. cit.*, p 328.

38. *ibid.*, pp 326–7.

39. The division into the three political categories was based on the respondents' own assessment of their ideological position, their voting behaviour at general elections, and their stated attitude to two key political issues: the legitimacy of positive discrimination as a form of social engineering and whether social policy should be based on the notion of equality of opportunity. By these criteria, 24 per cent of the sample was categorised left wing, 65.5 per cent politically centrist (Liberal to centre Labour) and 10.5 per cent right wing.

40. DES, *Adult Education: A Plan for Development* (HMSO, 1973), pp 71–2.

41. *ibid.*, p 72–4.

42. *ibid.*, p 72.

43. *ibid.*, p 73.

44. *ibid.*, pp 74–6.

45. *ibid.*, pp 77–81.

46. *ibid.*, para. 4, p x.

47. *ibid.*, pp 75–6.

48. See note 39 above.

49. See R. Fieldhouse, *Adult Education and the Cold War* (University of Leeds, 1985).